Fitzgerald

GW00384288

Lang**Syne**

PUBLISHING

WRITING *to* REMEMBER

Lang**Syne**

PUBLISHING

WRITING *to* REMEMBER

E-mail: info@lang-syne.co.uk

Distributed in the Republic of Ireland by Portfolio Group,
Kilbarrack Ind. Est. Kilbarrack, Dublin 5.
T:00353(01) 839 4918 F:00353(01) 839 5826
sales@portfoliogroup.ie
www.portfoliogroup.ie

Design by Dorothy Meikle   Printed by Ricoh Print Scotland

© Lang Syne Publishers Ltd 2013

ISBN 978-1-85217-254-1

Fitzgerald

MOTTO:
Crom-a-boo.

CREST:
A monkey.

NAME variations include:
MacGerailt *(Gaelic)*
FitzGerald
Fitz-Gerald
Gerald
Geralds
Geraldine

Chapter one:
Origins of Irish surnames

**According to an old saying, there are two types of Irish –
those who actually are Irish and those who wish they were.**

This sentiment is only one example of the allure that the
high romance and drama of the proud nation's history holds
for thousands of people scattered across the world today.

It's a sad fact, however, that the vast majority of Irish
surnames are found far beyond Irish shores, rather than on
the Emerald Isle itself.

The population stood at around eight million souls in
1841, but today it stands at fewer than six million.

This is mainly a tragic consequence of the potato
famine, also known as the Great Hunger, which devastated
Ireland between 1845 and 1849.

The Irish peasantry had become almost wholly reliant
for basic sustenance on the potato, first introduced from the
Americas in the seventeenth century.

When the crop was hit by a blight, at least 800,000
people starved to death while an estimated two million
others were forced to seek a new life far from their native
shores – particularly in America, Canada, and Australia.

The effects of the potato blight continued until about
1851, by which time a firm pattern of emigration had
become established.

Ireland's loss, however, was to the gain of the countries in which the immigrants settled, contributing enormously, as their descendants do today, to the well being of the nations in which their forefathers settled.

But those who were forced through dire circumstance to establish a new life in foreign parts never forgot their roots, or the proud heritage and traditions of the land that gave them birth.

Nor do their descendants.

It is a heritage that is inextricably bound up in the colourful variety of Irish names themselves – and the origin and history of these names forms an integral part of the vibrant drama that is the nation's history, one of both glorious fortune and tragic misfortune.

This history is well documented, and one of the most important and fascinating of the earliest sources are *The Annals of the Four Masters*, compiled between 1632 and 1636 by four friars at the Franciscan Monastery in County Donegal.

Compiled from earlier sources, and purporting to go back to the Biblical Deluge, much of the material takes in the mythological origins and history of Ireland and the Irish.

This includes tales of successive waves of invaders and settlers such as the Fomorians, the Partholonians, the Nemedians, the Fir Bolgs, the Tuatha De Danann, and the Laigain.

Of particular interest are the *Milesian Genealogies*,

because the majority of Irish clans today claim a descent from either Heremon, Ir, or Heber – three of the sons of Milesius, a king of what is now modern day Spain.

These sons invaded Ireland in the second millennium B.C, apparently in fulfilment of a mysterious prophecy received by their father.

This Milesian lineage is said to have ruled Ireland for nearly 3,000 years, until the island came under the sway of England's King Henry II in 1171 following what is known as the Cambro-Norman invasion.

This is an important date not only in Irish history in general, but for the effect the invasion subsequently had for Irish surnames.

'Cambro' comes from the Welsh, and 'Cambro-Norman' describes those Welsh knights of Norman origin who invaded Ireland.

But they were invaders who stayed, inter-marrying with the native Irish population and founding their own proud dynasties that bore Cambro-Norman names such as Archer, Barbour, Brannagh, Fitzgerald, Fitzgibbon, Fleming, Joyce, Plunkett, and Walsh – to name only a few.

These 'Cambro-Norman' surnames that still flourish throughout the world today form one of the three main categories in which Irish names can be placed – those of Gaelic-Irish, Cambro-Norman, and Anglo-Irish.

Previous to the Cambro-Norman invasion of the twelfth century, and throughout the earlier invasions and settlement of those wild bands of sea rovers known as the Vikings in the eighth and ninth centuries, the population of the island was relatively small, and it was normal for a person to be identified through the use of only a forename.

But as population gradually increased and there were many more people with the same forename, surnames were adopted to distinguish one person, or one community, from another.

Individuals identified themselves with their own particular tribe, or 'tuath', and this tribe – that also became known as a clann, or clan – took its name from some distinguished ancestor who had founded the clan.

The Gaelic-Irish form of the name Kelly, for example, is Ó Ceallaigh, or O'Kelly, indicating descent from an original 'Ceallaigh', with the 'O' denoting 'grandson of.' The name was later anglicised to Kelly.

The prefix 'Mac' or 'Mc', meanwhile, as with the clans of the Scottish Highlands, denotes 'son of.'

Although the Irish clans had much in common with their Scottish counterparts, one important difference lies in what are known as 'septs', or branches, of the clan.

Septs of Scottish clans were groups who often bore an entirely different name from the clan name but were under the clan's protection.

In Ireland, septs were groups that shared the same name and who could be found scattered throughout the four provinces of Ulster, Leinster, Munster, and Connacht.

The 'golden age' of the Gaelic-Irish clans, infused as their veins were with the blood of Celts, pre-dates the Viking invasions of the eighth and ninth centuries and the Norman invasion of the twelfth century, and the sacred heart of the country was the Hill of Tara, near the River Boyne, in County Meath.

Known in Gaelic as 'Teamhar na Rí', or Hill of Kings, it was the royal seat of the 'Ard Rí Éireann', or High King of Ireland, to whom the petty kings, or chieftains, from the island's provinces were ultimately subordinate.

It was on the Hill of Tara, beside a stone pillar known as the Irish 'Lia Fáil', or Stone of Destiny, that the High Kings were inaugurated and, according to legend, this stone would emit a piercing screech that could be heard all over Ireland when touched by the hand of the rightful king.

The Hill of Tara is today one of the island's main tourist attractions.

Opposition to English rule over Ireland, established in the wake of the Cambro-Norman invasion, broke out frequently and the harsh solution adopted by the powerful forces of the Crown was to forcibly evict the native Irish from their lands.

These lands were then granted to Protestant colonists, or 'planters', from Britain.

Many of these colonists, ironically, came from Scotland and were the descendants of the original 'Scotti', or 'Scots', who gave their name to Scotland after migrating there in the fifth century A.D., from the north of Ireland.

Colonisation entailed harsh penal laws being imposed on the majority of the native Irish population, stripping them practically of all of their rights.

The Crown's main bastion in Ireland was Dublin and its environs, known as the Pale, and it was the dispossessed peasantry who lived outside this Pale, desperately striving to eke out a meagre living.

It was this that gave rise to the modern-day expression of someone or something being 'beyond the pale'.

Attempts were made to stamp out all aspects of the ancient Gaelic-Irish culture, to the extent that even to bear a Gaelic-Irish name was to invite discrimination.

This is why many Gaelic-Irish names were anglicised with, for example, and noted above, Ó Ceallaigh, or O'Kelly, being anglicised to Kelly.

Succeeding centuries have seen strong revivals of Gaelic-Irish consciousness, however, and this has led to many families reverting back to the original form of their name, while the language itself is frequently found on the fluent tongues of an estimated 90,000 to 145,000 of the island's population.

Ireland's turbulent history of religious and political strife is one that lasted well into the twentieth century, a landmark century that saw the partition of the island into the twenty-six counties of the independent Republic of

Ireland, or Eire, and the six counties of Northern Ireland, or Ulster.

Dublin, originally founded by Vikings, is now a vibrant and truly cosmopolitan city while the proud city of Belfast is one of the jewels in the crown of Ulster.

It was Saint Patrick who first brought the light of Christianity to Ireland in the fifth century A.D.

Interpretations of this Christian message have varied over the centuries, often leading to bitter sectarian conflict – but the many intricately sculpted Celtic Crosses found all over the island are symbolic of a unity that crosses the sectarian divide.

It is an image that fuses the 'old gods' of the Celts with Christianity.

All the signs from the early years of this new millennium indicate that sectarian strife may soon become a thing of the past – with the Irish and their many kinsfolk across the world, be they Protestant or Catholic, finding common purpose in the rich tapestry of their shared heritage.

Chapter two:

A noble dynasty

Although they first arrived in Ireland in the late twelfth century as invaders, the Fitzgeralds soon became established as one of the island's most powerful dynasties and assimilated the habits and culture of the nation to such an extent that they were described as 'more Irish than the Irish themselves.'

Their identification with their new homeland and proud sense of independence, however, would in subsequent centuries lead them into bitter and bloody conflict with the English Crown and setbacks in their fortunes.

The most common form of the name today is 'Fitzgerald', although the form 'FitzGerald' has also been in use for several centuries and is still found today, as we will see in Chapter four.

For the sake of consistency in the following two chapters of this historical narrative of the family, however, 'Fitzgerald' is the style adopted.

The 'Fitz' prefix simply denotes 'son of', while the Norman personal name 'Gerald' has truly martial connotations stemming as it does from the Germanic 'geri', meaning 'spear', and 'wald', meaning 'rule.'

No more fitting name could have been assumed by this

family who first arrived on the shores of England in the military retinue of William, Duke of Normandy.

Defeating the hastily assembled forces of Harold II, the last Anglo-Saxon king of England, at the battle of Hastings in 1066, the Fitzgeralds and other leading Norman supporters of the Duke were rewarded with lands – with a branch of the Fitzgeralds settling in Wales.

The roots of how they subsequently crossed the sea to Ireland as part of a mighty Norman invasion force can be traced back to the fact that it was far from being a unified nation.

It was split up into territories ruled over by squabbling and competing chieftains who ruled as kings in their own right – and this inter-clan rivalry worked to the advantage of the invaders.

In a series of bloody conflicts one chieftain, or king, would occasionally gain the upper hand over his rivals, and by 1156 the most powerful was Muirchertach MacLochlainn, king of the powerful O'Neills.

The equally powerful Rory O'Connor, king of the province of Connacht, opposed him but he increased his power and influence by allying himself with Dermot MacMurrough, king of Leinster.

MacLochlainn and MacMurrough were aware that the main key to the kingdom of Ireland was the thriving trading port of Dublin that had been established by invading Vikings, or Ostmen, in 852 A.D.

Dublin was taken by the combined forces of the Leinster and Connacht kings, but when MacLochlainn died the Dubliners rose up in revolt and overthrew the unpopular MacMurrough.

A triumphant Rory O'Connor entered Dublin and was later inaugurated as Ard Rí, but MacMurrough refused to accept defeat.

He appealed for help from England's Henry II in unseating O'Connor, an act that was to radically affect the future course of Ireland's fortunes.

The English monarch agreed to help MacMurrough, but distanced himself from direct action by delegating his Norman subjects in Wales such as the Fitzgeralds with the task.

MacMurrough rallied powerful barons such as Maurice Fitzgerald to his cause, along with Gilbert de Clare, Earl of Pembroke, also known as Strongbow.

As an inducement to Strongbow, MacMurrough offered him the hand of his beautiful young daughter, Aife, in marriage, with the further sweetener to the deal that he would take over the province of Leinster on MacMurrough's death.

The mighty Norman war machine soon moved into action, and so fierce and disciplined was their onslaught on the forces of Rory O'Connor and his allies that by 1171 they had re-captured Dublin, in the name of MacMurrough, and other strategically important territories.

Henry II now began to take cold feet over the venture, realising that he may have created a rival in the form of a separate Norman kingdom in Ireland – he landed on the island, near Waterford, at the head of a large army in October of 1171 with the aim of curbing the power of his Cambro-Norman barons.

Protracted war between the king and his barons was averted, however, when the barons submitted to the royal will, promising homage and allegiance in return for holding the territories they had conquered in the king's name.

English dominion over Ireland was ratified through the Treaty of Windsor of 1175.

Maurice Fitzgerald and his retainers had fought under the banner of the mighty Strongbow and had been rewarded by him with lands in Munster, ownership of which was confirmed after they swore fealty to the English Crown.

But it was not long before the family divided into two main branches: one branch ruled in Munster as the Earls of Desmond while Leinster was a fiefdom of the Earls of Kildare and subsequent Dukes of Leinster.

The dukedom of Leinster is still held by the family, while the title of the eldest son and heir is Marquess of Kildare.

The main stronghold of this branch of the Fitzgerald dynasty was originally a castle in Maynooth, in Co. Kildare, but estates were also held in Co. Waterford, where they built Carton House.

A magnificent townhouse was also built in Dublin; originally named Kildare House, it became Leinster House when the Earl of Kildare was awarded his dukedom.

Sold by the family in the early years of the nineteenth century, it served for a time as the headquarters of the Royal Dublin Society before becoming the seat of the parliament of the Irish Free State in 1922.

It was bought outright by the government two years later, and today Leinster House serves as the parliament house of the Irish Republic.

Carton House, in Waterford, along with other properties, was also sold and the Leinster branch of the Fitzgeralds is now settled across the Irish Sea in England's rural Oxfordshire.

The main coat of arms displayed by the Fitzgeralds – or the Geraldines, as the dynasty of Fitzgeralds is known – is that of the Dukes of Leinster, and two strange legends are attached to their rather odd crest of a monkey with a collar around its middle.

One legend is that a young son of the family was taken by a monkey from his baby carriage and carried to the top of the family castle.

There was obviously great consternation, as it was feared the monkey would throw the child to the ground below – but after a time it carefully clambered back down and, placing the child back in his carriage, gave his nanny a sharp slap for having left the child unattended in the first place.

Another legend is that a monkey had rescued John Fitzgerald, 1st Earl of Kildare, from a fire when he was a baby – and this is held to explain one of the family mottoes of 'Not forgetful of a helping hand.'

The traditional motto of the Fitzgeralds, however, is 'Crom-a-boo', with Crom being a name of a family castle.

One explanation of the motto is that it means 'Crom forever', but the likeliest explanation is that it means 'Crom to victory', stemming from the Irish Gaelic word 'a buadh', signifying 'victory.'

As they readily assimilated the native Irish culture, the Fitzgeralds became more 'Hiberno-Norman' (Irish–Norman) rather than their original Cambro-Norman.

They also looked down disdainfully on those Anglo-Norman settlers, adventurers, and Crown officials who flocked to the island in the years following the original invasion.

This was destined to lead them into serious conflict with the Crown, and one infamous example comes from February of 1565 when the forces of the Fitzgerald Earl of Desmond met with the rival forces of the Butler Earl of Ormonde at the battle of Affane, near Lismore.

The battle, one of the last 'private' battles to have been fought in either Ireland or on the British mainland, stemmed from family feuds between the proud and powerful Fitzgerald and Butler families, and resulted in a resounding defeat for the Earl of Desmond.

A furious Queen Elizabeth, who was certainly not amused at two of her noble subjects engaging in private war, had the Earl of Desmond and two of his brothers cast into the Tower of London, after the Earl of Ormonde, her cousin, convinced her he had been blameless in the affair.

Although it could not have been foreseen at the time, this was to sow the seeds of two cataclysmic rebellions, known as the Desmond Rebellions, which still stand out among the bloodstained pages of Ireland's history.

Chapter three:
Revolt and terror

A policy of 'plantation' of loyal Protestants in Ireland had first begun during the reign of England's Henry VIII, whose religious Reformation effectively outlawed the practice of the Roman Catholic faith in his domains.

This practice of settling Protestants in Ireland, combined with attempts to stamp the Crown's authority on the island continued under the reign of Elizabeth, culminating in an attempt to curb the power of feudal lords such as the Fitzgeralds by appointing Crown commissioners to their territories and effectively de-militarising them.

With the Fitzgerald Earl of Desmond and his two brothers held in the grim confines of the Tower of London following the debacle of the battle of Affane, the leadership of the family in Munster fell to James Fitzmaurice Fitzgerald, described as 'captain general' of the Fitzgeralds.

Resolving to curb the encroachments of the Crown on the Fitzgerald territory and to strike a blow into the bargain against the rival Earl of Ormonde, Fitzmaurice effectively declared war on the Crown when, supported by native Irish clans such as the MacCarthys, O'Sullivans, and O'Keefes, he descended on an English colony south of Cork in June of 1569.

Cork city itself was then attacked, followed by a siege of

the Earl of Ormonde's stronghold of Kilkenny the following month.

Fitzmaurice had cleverly exploited divisions in the Butler Earl of Ormonde's family by enlisting the support of two of his brothers while the Earl was in London; he soon returned, however, and swung his family around in support of the Crown.

Henry Sidney, Lord Deputy of Ireland, reacted to the sudden insurrection by mobilising troops in the island itself and enlisting the aid of more troops rapidly despatched to meet the emergency from England.

Sidney appointed Humphrey Gilbert as governor of Munster, and under his direction the province was devastated and hundreds of innocent civilians summarily put to the sword.

One of the many terror tactics he employed to cow both the civilian population and the rebels was to set up a grisly corridor of decapitated heads outside the entrances to his military camps.

As Munster groaned under this terror and became a virtual wasteland, Fitzmaurice and his allies resorted to daring guerrilla tactics launched from their base in the Kerry mountains, but they were no match for the superior might of the Crown.

Many of his allies were forced into surrender, and in February of 1573 Fitzmaurice himself surrendered after promise of a pardon.

The First Desmond Rebellion had been quashed, with Fitzmaurice leaving for France in 1575, but the embers of rebellion were still there – only awaiting the spark that launched the Second Desmond Rebellion.

James Fitzmaurice Fitzgerald returned from his exile on the continent in 1579.

He had certainly not been idle during his four years of exile; as a devout Roman Catholic he had enlisted the aid of no less than the Pope and King Phillip II of Spain in what became a crusade to crush the power of the English Crown once and for all in Ireland.

With the Pope's blessing, troops, and money, in addition to a number of Spanish and Italian troops, he landed at Smerwick, in Co. Kerry, on July 18 of 1579, intent on the invasion of Munster.

The Earl of Desmond and his brothers had earlier been released from their captivity in the Tower of London and one these brothers, John Fitzgerald, rallied to his kinsman Fitzmaurice's desperate cause.

The rebellion would have been left leaderless had John Fitzgerald not joined the rebels, because Fitzmaurice was killed in a skirmish only a few weeks later.

John Fitzgerald assumed the leadership, but his brother, the Earl of Desmond, rather reluctantly assumed this mantle a short time later after the Crown declared him a traitor.

It was a role that would cost him and his family dear.

The rebels struck a number of stunning blows against

the Crown under the Earl's leadership, including the sacking of the towns of Youghal and Kinsale, but by the summer of 1580 they were mainly on the defensive, despite the rebellion having spread into Leinster.

Reinforcements to the rebel cause arrived in September of 1580 in the form of troops despatched by the Pope; but they surrendered and were massacred to the last man only a short time after they landed in Kerry after being besieged in a fort at Dun an Oir.

The rebellion dragged on, however, only reaching an exhausted conclusion in November of 1583 when the Earl of Desmond was killed near Tralee, in Kerry.

Adding to the ignominy of his defeat, his severed head was sent to Queen Elizabeth, while his body was displayed on the walls of Cork city.

The fortunes of the Fitzgerald Earls of Desmond were now all but totally destroyed, and Munster itself now lay devastated after years of warfare, famine, and plague.

England's grip on the island tightened in subsequent years, particularly through the Cromwellian conquest of 1649.

A series of harsh penal laws against Catholics were passed, including, in 1695, legislation that restricted their rights to bear arms, in education, and even in the ownership of horses.

By 1704 Catholics had to submit to a series of humiliating loyalty 'tests', before even being considered for any form of public office, while in 1728 an Act was passed that withdrew their right to vote.

This only served to stoke the fires of a series of rebellions, one of the most memorable of which was the Rising of 1798 – one in which Lord Edward Fitzgerald, 5th son of the 1st Duke of Leinster played a prominent role.

The Rising was sparked off by a fusion of sectarian and agrarian unrest and a burning desire for political reform that had been shaped by the French revolutionary slogan of 'liberty, equality, and fraternity.'

A movement known as the United Irishmen had come into existence, embracing both middle-class intellectuals and the oppressed peasantry, and Lord Edward was among its leaders.

Despite attempts by the British government to concede a degree of agrarian and political reform, it was a case of far too little and much too late, and by 1795 the United Irishmen, were receiving help from France – Britain's enemy.

A French invasion fleet was despatched to Ireland in December of 1796, but it was scattered by storms off Bantry Bay.

Two years later, in the summer of 1798, rebellion broke out on the island.

The first flames of revolt were fanned in Ulster, but soon died out, only to be replaced by a much more serious conflagration centred mainly in Co. Wexford.

Victory was achieved at the battle of Oulart Hill, followed by another victory at the battle of Three Rocks, but the peasant army was no match for the 20,000 troops or so that descended on Wexford.

Defeat followed at the battle of Vinegar Hill on 21 June 1798, followed by another decisive defeat five days later at Kilcumney Hill.

Earlier, in March, an arrest warrant had been issued for the leaders of the United Irishmen, including the 35-year-old Lord Edward Fitzgerald, who had joined the movement two years before and was one of its leading conspirators.

He was captured in May after his hiding place in a house in Dublin was betrayed to the authorities – but his capture did not come without a fight on his part.

He had been lying in bed recovering from fever when the arresting officers burst into the room.

Stabbing one of them and killing another, he was shot in the shoulder and clubbed to the ground with rifle butts.

He was taken to Newgate Prison, in London, where he died on June 4, after being refused proper medical treatment for his severe wounds; his estates were confiscated, but restored to the family in 1819.

Lord Edward's wife, Lady Pamela Fitzgerald, had also been an enthusiastic supporter of Ireland's republican cause, and she was forced to flee into exile, dying in Paris in 1831.

Chapter four:
On the world stage

Far from the tumult and strife of earlier centuries, generations of Fitzgeralds and their namesakes the FitzGeralds have brought fame and honour to the name in a wide variety of pursuits.

Beginning her acting career on the Dublin stage in 1932, **Geraldine Fitzgerald** went on to become an Academy Award-nominated actress.

Born in Greystones, Co. Wicklow, in 1913, she moved to London two years after her stage debut in Dublin to appear in a number of British films, including the 1937 *The Mill on the Floss*.

Success followed later on Broadway and the Hollywood screen, and she received an Academy Award nomination for Best Supporting actress in 1939 for her role in *Wuthering Heights*.

Other movies followed, including *Shining Victory*, from 1941, *Ten North Frederick*, from 1961, and *Arthur 2* in 1988.

A cousin of the Australian novelist Nevil Shute and the mother of contemporary film director Michael Lindsay-Hogg, she was honoured with a star on the Hollywood Walk of Fame before her death in 2005.

She was also a great aunt of the contemporary English actress **Tara Fitzgerald**, born in Sussex in 1967 and who has appeared in films that include *Sirens*, with High Grant, and the 1996 *Brassed Off*, in addition to a number of television roles.

Also on the stage, **Barry Fitzgerald**, born William Joseph Shields in Dublin in 1888, was the Irish actor who also trod the boards of the Dublin stage before appearing in the 1930 Alfred Hitchcock film version of the Irish playwright Sean O'Casey's *Juno and the Paycock*.

His many other acclaimed film appearances included *The Quiet Man*, *The Long Voyage Home*, and *How Green Was My Valley*, while in 1944 he achieved the rare distinction of being nominated for both Best Actor and Best Supporting Actor for the same role in *Going My Way* – taking the Oscar for Best Supporting Actor. He died in 1961.

Born in Newport News, Virginia, in 1917, **Ella Fitzgerald** will be long remembered as the 'First Lady of Song', and one of the most influential jazz singers of the twentieth century.

In a recording career that spanned 57 years, she was the winner of 13 Grammy Awards and was awarded the National Medal of Art by Ronald Reagan and the Presidential Medal of Freedom by George H.W. Bush before her death in 1996.

Born into humble circumstances, 'Lady Ella' was responsible for a number of memorable quotations in her lifetime, including: 'It isn't where you come from, it's where you're going that counts.'

From charismatic actors and singers, the Fitzgeralds have also produced a fair share of charismatic politicians, not least **John 'Honey Fitz' Fitzgerald**, the American politician who was the maternal grandfather, through his daughter Rose, of U.S. President **John Fitzgerald Kennedy**.

Born in Boston, Massachusetts, of Irish stock in 1863, he became a prominent Democratic Party wheeler and dealer in his native city. Renowned for his charm and honeyed 'gift of the gab' he was elected Mayor of Boston on two separate occasions.

In 'Honey Fitz's' ancestral home of Ireland, **Alexis FitzGerald** was the Fine Gael party politician, solicitor, and lecturer in economics who served for a time in the early 1980s as a special advisor to the Taoiseach (Prime Minister) of the Irish Republic, while his nephew **Alexis FitzGerald Jnr.**, is a former Fine Gael politician and a former Lord Mayor of Dublin.

The Taoiseach who Alexis Fitzgerald snr. served as a special advisor was **Garret FitzGerald**, born in Dublin in 1926 and who served two terms as Taoiseach.

A member of Fine Gael and its leader from between 1977 and 1987, he is now, at the time of writing, Chancellor of the National University of Ireland.

His father, **Desmond FitzGerald**, was the first Minister for External Affairs for the Irish Free State.

Back across the Atlantic, **Frank Fitzgerald**, born in

1885 was the Republican politician who served two terms as governor of Michigan, while in Queensland, Australia, **Thomas Henry FitzGerald**, born in Carrickmacross, Co. Monaghan, in 1824, became a pioneer of sugar cane farming and prominent politician in his adopted homeland.

He also founded the town of Innisfail, in Queensland.

Also in Australia, **Captain Charles Fitzgerald**, born in 1794, served from 1848 to 1855 as governor of Western Australia, where the town of Geraldton is named after him.

Patrick J. Fitzgerald, born in 1960 in Brooklyn, New York, is a prominent U.S. Attorney and federal prosecutor with the U.S. Department of Justice.

In the creative world of literature, Francis Scott Fitzgerald, better known as **F. Scott Fitzgerald**, is regarded as having been one of the greatest writers of the twentieth century.

Born in St. Paul, Minnesota, in 1896, his first novel, *This Side of Paradise*, was published in 1920, followed by *The Beauty and Damned*, *The Great Gatsby*, and the 1934 *Tender is the Night*.

He married Zelda Sayre in 1900, and she is thought to have been the character Nicole Diver in *Tender is the Night*. The couple had a difficult relationship, and this is reflected in Zelda's autobiographical novel *Save Me The Waltz*.

She died in a fire in a mental hospital in 1948, eight years after her husband's death.

Born in Price, Utah, in 1907, **John D. Fitzgerald** was

the American author whose works included *Papa Married a Mormon* and *The Great Brain* series of popular children's books, while **Francis FitzGerald**, born in 1940, is the American journalist and author whose best known work is her 1972 *Fire in the Lake: The Vietnamese and the Americans in Vietnam*, for which she won both a Pulitzer Prize and a National Book Award.

She is also a half-sister of the 1960s supermodel Penelope Tree.

Judith Fitzgerald, born in Toronto in 1952, is an acclaimed Canadian journalist and poet, while **Penelope Fitzgerald**, who was born in 1916 and died in 2000, was a celebrated English novelist, biographer, and poet.

Edward FitzGerald, born in Suffolk in 1809, was the writer responsible for the first English translation of the *Rubáiyát of Omar Khayyám*.

In the world of art, **Lionel LeMoine Fitzgerald**, who was born in Winnipeg in 1890 and died in 1956, was the Canadian artist who was a member of the country's famous artistic elite known as the Group of Seven, and later a founder member of its successor, the Canadian Group of Painters.

In the highly competitive world of sport, **Ciaran Fitzgerald**, born in 1952, is the former Irish rugby union hooker who captained his nation to the Triple Crown in 1983 and 1985; he was also the Irish national rugby coach from 1990 to 1992.

In Australian rules football, **Ryan 'Fitzy' Fitzgerald**, born in 1976, is a former player with South Adelaide Football Club and now a media personality, while in American football **Larry Fitzgerald**, born in Minneapolis in 1983, is the wide receiver who, at the time of writing, plays for the Arizona Cardinals.

Also at the time of writing his brother, **Marcus Fitzgerald**, plays wide receiver for Marshall University.

In the fast paced and bruising game of camogie – the women's version of the Irish sport of hurling – a leading player is **Pamela Fitzgerald**, born in Cork in 1984.

In the world of science, **George FitzGerald**, born in Dublin in 1851, was a physicist who carried out pioneering work in electromagnetism, while **Gerald FitzGerald**, 11th Earl of Kildare, is reputed to have resorted to supernatural means to explore the natural world.

Born in 1525, he was educated on the Continent, and it was here that his interest in alchemy, the attempt to turn base metal into gold, was first aroused.

Returning to the Kildare stronghold of Kilkea Castle he soon earned himself the feared name of 'The Wizard Earl' because of the mysterious experiments he carried out behind the castle walls.

Said to have possessed magical powers, he died in 1585 and, according to ancient legend, his ghost returns to haunt the castle every seven years, mounted on a silver-shod white horse.

Key dates in Ireland's history from the first settlers to the formation of the Irish Republic:

circa 7000 B.C.	Arrival and settlement of Stone Age people.
circa 3000 B.C.	Arrival of settlers of New Stone Age period.
circa 600 B.C.	First arrival of the Celts.
200 A.D.	Establishment of Hill of Tara, Co. Meath, as seat of the High Kings.
circa 432 A.D.	Christian mission of St. Patrick.
800-920 A.D.	Invasion and subsequent settlement of Vikings.
1002 A.D.	Brian Boru recognised as High King.
1014	Brian Boru killed at battle of Clontarf.
1169-1170	Cambro-Norman invasion of the island.
1171	Henry II claims Ireland for the English Crown.
1366	Statutes of Kilkenny ban marriage between native Irish and English.
1529-1536	England's Henry VIII embarks on religious Reformation.
1536	Earl of Kildare rebels against the Crown.
1541	Henry VIII declared King of Ireland.
1558	Accession to English throne of Elizabeth I.
1565	Battle of Affane.
1569-1573	First Desmond Rebellion.
1579-1583	Second Desmond Rebellion.
1594-1603	Nine Years War.
1606	Plantation' of Scottish and English settlers.
1607	Flight of the Earls.
1632-1636	Annals of the Four Masters compiled.
1641	Rebellion over policy of plantation and other grievances.
1649	Beginning of Cromwellian conquest.
1688	Flight into exile in France of Catholic Stuart monarch James II as Protestant Prince William of Orange invited to take throne of England along with his wife, Mary.
1689	William and Mary enthroned as joint monarchs; siege of Derry.
1690	Jacobite forces of James defeated by William at battle of the Boyne (July) and Dublin taken.

1691	Athlone taken by William; Jacobite defeats follow at Aughrim, Galway, and Limerick; conflict ends with Treaty of Limerick (October) and Irish officers allowed to leave for France.
1695	Penal laws introduced to restrict rights of Catholics; banishment of Catholic clergy.
1704	Laws introduced constricting rights of Catholics in landholding and public office.
1728	Franchise removed from Catholics.
1791	Foundation of United Irishmen republican movement.
1796	French invasion force lands in Bantry Bay.
1798	Defeat of Rising in Wexford and death of United Irishmen leaders Wolfe Tone and Lord Edward Fitzgerald.
1800	Act of Union between England and Ireland.
1803	Dublin Rising under Robert Emmet.
1829	Catholics allowed to sit in Parliament.
1845-1849	The Great Hunger: thousands starve to death as potato crop fails and thousands more emigrate.
1856	Phoenix Society founded.
1858	Irish Republican Brotherhood established.
1873	Foundation of Home Rule League.
1893	Foundation of Gaelic League.
1904	Foundation of Irish Reform Association.
1913	Dublin strikes and lockout.
1916	Easter Rising in Dublin and proclamation of an Irish Republic.
1917	Irish Parliament formed after Sinn Fein election victory.
1919-1921	War between Irish Republican Army and British Army.
1922	Irish Free State founded, while six northern counties remain part of United Kingdom as Northern Ireland, or Ulster; civil war up until 1923 between rival republican groups.
1949	Foundation of Irish Republic after all remaining constitutional links with Britain are severed.